Charles Gershom Fall

Village Sketch

And Other Poems

Charles Gershom Fall

Village Sketch
And Other Poems

ISBN/EAN: 9783744705332

Printed in Europe, USA, Canada, Australia, Japan

Cover: Foto ©Thomas Meinert / pixelio.de

More available books at **www.hansebooks.com**

A VILLAGE SKETCH

AND

OTHER POEMS

BY

CHARLES G. FALL

———

BOSTON

CUPPLES, UPHAM & COMPANY

Old Corner Bookstore

1886

INTRODUCTION.

WHO loves not laughing brooks and shady
    dells?
Who loves not sparkling draughts from moss-
    grown wells?
Loves not the song of birds, of lisping
    trees?
The new-mown hay that scents the evening
    breeze?
What fervent heart loves not a rural home?
Loves not at dusk through violet vales to
    roam?
When Autumn tints the leaves with sunset
    rays,
The cattle round the farmer's doorstep graze,

The reapers bind in sheaves the golden
    grain,
Big oxen homeward tug the creaking wain,
What eye but brightens at the festive sight?
What maiden's heart but throbs with fond
    delight,
When harvest moons distil their crystal gleams,
When dingy lanterns deck the dusky beams,
The barn is piled with russet sheaves of corn
Kind Nature empties from her sumptuous
    horn ?
What peals of laughter, roistering shouts we
    hear
When blushing Ruth unhusks the speckled
    ear,
Contending swains demand the forfeit due !
'Tis here that tell-tale tongues and eyes speak
    true !
The sun that browns their faces warms their
    hearts ;

The breeze that steels their sinews scorns all
    arts !
As free as air, contented as the roe,
They eat the bread that thrifty hands can sow ;
No debts nor pains, some honey in the hive,
A simple country life's the life to live.

A VILLAGE SKETCH.

'TIS evening. Night's majestic, full-orbed
    Queen,
High in the boundless empyrean seen,
Is silvering o'er the river and the sea,
The verdant hillside and the fragrant lea.
See, where look down the silent stars above,
Calm, glowing, constant, like true eyes of love !
The firmament,—a vast, inverted shield,
With gems bestudding all its azure field,—
How luminous with shimmering, starry dust!
The rain is o'er. The fleeting, fitful gust
That shook the glistening opals from the
    leaves
Has died away. How Ocean's bosom heaves

And falls with peaceful breathings, long and
    deep,
As though some wearied giant lay asleep!
His breath, see how it floats along the river's
    side,
As would some serpent o'er its surface glide !
It creeps along the valley, skirts the hill,
Obscures the bridge, enfolds the drowsy mill,
Earth's dusky form in fleecy robe invests,
While Ocean's Sister in soft slumber rests.

Silence is Queen. The toils of day are done.
The kine, returning with the setting sun,
Have now lain down, embowered in fragrant
    sleep.
Beside them nestle soft-eyed, white-flecked
    sheep,—
Meek, silent symbols of that loved content
To rural innocence from Heaven sent !
The farmer, dragging home his heavy feet,

His children run with outstretched hands to
greet.
The lowing ox, the merry milkmaid's song,
She trilled in cadence as she tripped along,
The twittering swallow,—these are heard no
more.
Now chirps the cricket 'neath the farmer's
door;
The owl, night's herald, pipes his plaintive
wail;
While twilight draws across the fields her veil.

Beside yon road with stately maples lined,
Whose trunks are now with russet woodbine
twined,
Not far from where those arching highways
meet,—
Once trod by solemn, Puritanic feet,—
An ancient, gambrel meeting-house is seen.
It stands within the forest-templed green,

Across whose velvet lawn loud rustics play
While twilight lengthens out the loitering day.

The village parson lives within a stride.
His joy it is with patient care to guide
His scattered flock along the narrow way
That leads from darkness unto endless day.
'Tis he that cheers the lonely widow's lot,
Reminds her God a sparrow ne'er forgot ;
'Tis he that meets the beggar at his door,
Divides with him a spare and simple store ;
He grasps the tottering drunkard by the hand,
Points out where surging breakers sweep the
    strand ;
He cheers the downcast, holds the proud in
    check
With spectres of the soul's eternal wreck.
I see him now, I see his generous face,
His stooping form, his grave and gracious
    pace,

His locks that float like snow adown the
    wind,
His kindly smile that speaks the saintly
    mind.
Yes! now I hear his soft, approving word,
So often longed for since, so seldom heard;
I feel the tender pressure of that hand,
No other like it since in all the land!
In reverie, see the stealing tear-drop gleam
When told that I must shatter home's bright
    dream,
Must woo the genii of some other sphere,
Where Fame's proud conquests are more sure
    than here.

Farewell! farewell forever, reverend shade!
Thy form Affection's hand long since has laid
Beside the partner of thy joys and woes,
Near where yon mourning, murmuring river
    flows,

Amidst thy children, 'midst the friends loved
    best,
Gone on before to their eternal rest ;
Beneath the willows on the silent shore
Thy saintly shade shall haunt forever more.
Time, like yon leaden river, still shall flow,
Lethean mists dispel the long ago ;
But never, never, till life's stream runs dry,
Shall fade your bright example from mine eye!

Near by, o'ershadowed by a monarch oak,
'Gainst which the storms for centuries have
    broke,
Whose giant, gnarled arms, extending high,
The woodman and the whirlwind both defy ;
Across a brook that bounds with break-neck
    haste
To join the river's deeply rolling waste,
The village blacksmith swings his ponderous
    sledge.

His the true hand that gives the scythe its
    edge,
Builds the broad wagon, rims its rumbling
    wheel,
He fashions tools, and shapes the stubborn
    steel.
With beard unshorn and curling, crispy hair,
With sleeves uprolled and swarthy chest laid
    bare,
With brawny arms, with strength though little
    grace,
His blazing forge reflected on his face,
He seems the counterpart of that grim god
Who, under Ætna, War's mailed horses shod.
He is withal so gentle, e'en so kind,
When school lets out, the children you will find,
With open mouth and bright, astonished eye,
Watching the flashes from his anvil fly,
Or playing quoits with horseshoes on the floor,
Or begging one to hang above some door.

What place is there sere Manhood more ad-
    mires
Than where Ambition's day-dream first as-
    pires?
Where Childhood's rambling energies are
    taught
To chase, instead of butterflies, winged
    thought?
The school-house, rosy red, stands all alone
Beside the road with purple thistles grown.
Here Learning dons its solemn stole each
    year,
Here thirst for knowledge conquers winter's
    fear.
The master enters, tall and gaunt and thin,
A stripling seems, with down upon his chin.
At first, a cordial, welcome word is said,
In choral unison the Bible read ;
Then all repeat our Saviour's hallowed prayer
Which like frankincense fills the breathless air.

The child who sips such crystal fountains
    first
For passion's pools can ne'er acquire a thirst.

How school-day scenes revisit Memory's sight,
Our eyes dilated at the athlete's might,
The runner's flying feet, the wrestler's skill,
The boxer's leaden hand and iron will!
Who loves not, loves not now, the well-thrown
    quoit,
The flashing oar, the flying ball's exploit?
Whose eyes glow not to see the bully thrown,
The coward scorned, the brave receive his
    own?

Has Age more wisdom than the school-boy
    knew,
That Honor's chaplets only crown the true?
True worth prevails, prevails where Truth
    holds sway;

Where Freedom holds, through Treason's
    toils, her way ;
Where War's wild echoes clash, its thunders
    roar,
Its lightnings crash and screaming bomb-
    shells soar ;
Prevails where heaven-born genius draws the
    line
Admiring ages call the form divine ;
Where clarion lips proclaim the living word
Our sons unborn shall wish their sons had
    heard.

Within yon vine-clad walls the churchyard
    lies :
Who walks its narrow paths with tearless eyes ?
Above yon velvet mound still rests the bier
Has borne so many footsore travellers here.
As we approach (alas ! familiar scene),
We see a long procession cross the green ; —

The drooping widow see, in mourning weeds.
Oh, how her heart with bitter anguish bleeds!
How, how her children clutch her trembling
    hands,
Their thoughts, like spectres, haunting spirit-
    lands!
The brother see,—his idol dashed to earth!
The mother, too, — her gem of priceless
    worth
Now sparkles in her blessed Saviour's crown!
The father,—hopes ·like blossoms trodden
    down!
Across his path the roaring tempest's blast
Has swept, has left him, like some monarch
    oak,
Shorn of its branches, shattered, prostrate,
    broke.

The current of whose life has run so slow
No ripples have disturbed its peaceful flow?

Who, who's not seen some dear, some faithful
    heart
Transfixed by death's swift-winged, unerring
    dart?
How oft, how oft, must Memory recall
Some wasting form, wan face, some funeral
    pall!

I see a crumbling gateway open wide;
The villagers, I see them stand aside;
The sexton and the clergyman appear,
The bearers with the consecrated bier,
The laurel wreath a sister's hand had made,—
All, all now dim in twilight's deepening shade!
I see the shadowy figures pass along,—
The old, the young, the pale-faced, and the
    strong;
The men who knew his flaming falchion's
    might,
And loved him for his lofty love of right;

The life-long friend, who prized him, oh, so well,
And knew of golden hours no tongue could
    tell;
Grave women, who have seen the brow unbent
That through Wrong's armor gleaming arrows
    sent;
The child, whose face had caught the glowing
    smile
That oft stooped down her sorrows to beguile.
She laid those violets upon his shroud,
She knew the head, borne high, was never
    proud.
The cortège moves, with slow and measured
    tread.
In loving circle, with uncovered head,
We stand above the yawning, dreadful tomb
(That close Bastile, those walls of mouldering
    gloom!)
The dirge is chanted, the last prayer is said,
While immortelles we shower round his head.

The chains thou forgest, Death, with spirit
    hands,
Thy cruel chains outlast Cyclopean bands !
We turn and leave him, leave him there alone,
Our throats too stifled to express a moan ;
Yes, turn away our faces toward the night ;
No sun ! No moon ! No star nor ray of
    light !
Eternal winter whitens all the fields,
Hope's crystal spring no living water yields !

When limping Age descends the hill of life,
Footsore and jaded, weary with its strife,
Scarred like a Spartan, his last battle won,
Kind Nature covers with his shield her son.
Not so when ardent Manhood climbs the road,
No steep a hindrance and no pack a load :
If Fate's fell lightnings flash from summer
    skies,
He dies unseen, with none to close his eyes.

There is a lovely spot whose sun-kissed sod
I often sit beside : my Fancy's god
Is here enshrined.   It is the lonely mound
Where many a night (how hallowed is the
    ground !)
With reverent knee and glistening eye I've
    knelt,
In grief that filial hearts alone have felt.
The phantom-form that Imagery could draw
Is all the semblance Memory's eye e'er saw.
An eye of love ; of kind, unfelt command,
A soul that swept the strings from sweet to
    grand ;
A smile that Heaven to earth in pleasance
    brings ;
A voice as of the sparkling brook that sings
When rippling rills o'er plaintive pebbles play.

Ye everglades ! ye sprites, and elfin spray !
Ye changing vistas and ye dancing shades !

Ye templed groves and stately colonnades
Whose graceful pines their leafy arches raise
Where forest minstrels trill their hymns of
    praise !
Ye were her inspiration,— childhood's home,
Where Fancy with the wood-nymphs joyed to
    roam.

Would, would, my mother, thy lone child had
    known
Thy voice, thy smile and spirit long since
    flown !
Had felt thy loving arms around him twine,
Had seen thine eyes with affection's lustre
    shine!
Had felt thy magic wand of sympathy,
Been guided by thy star of piety !
Aye, caught the spark of thy heroic soul
That burned to have thy son love honor's
    goal !

Whene'er my eyelids drooped with childhood's
    toil,
Were books a nightmare, life a noisy broil,
Oh, could I on thy breast have laid my head!
Before the kiss was given, good-night was
    said,
Could I have lispt with thee my evening
    prayer!
Since disappointment was my bitter share,
Could I have shared with thee youth's load of
    care,
Could I have whispered in a mother's ear
The sorrows pride would let none other hear!

Hard by, but farther up yon brawling stream,
It tumbles o'er a dam in foaming cream ;
And, rushing round steep rocks, a maelstrom
    forms :
Here plaything boats are wrecked, as ships in
    storms.

'Tis here the dancing moon upon the spray
In dreams has figured many a silvery fay.
'Tis here, within the shadow of yon hill
Whose brow the moonlight kisses, stands the
      mill,
Among tall elms in garnet robes arrayed.
How once our fancies frolicked 'neath their
      shade !
The miller here from morn till e'en is found.
His honest face is known the country round ;
The merry twinkle of his laughing eye
Bespeaks a soul that seldom draws a sigh.
Do not his jests, his stories, often told,
Pass through the neighborhood like current
      gold ?
How oft the farmers, come to get their mail,
To catch the gossip, learn the latest tale,
How oft they linger round the miller's door !
Around the stove, within the village store,
Where quibblers don the robe Sam Adams
      wore,

Although the justice is the senate's chief,
The miller's wit oft brings the Law to grief.

Our life's a span! The chilling hand of Time,
That chokes the current of the climbing thyme,
That holds in icy grip the torrent's force,
Will dam, erelong, our feeble life blood's force.
The village worthies of the long ago,
Like withered leaves beneath the sheeted
 snow,
Are veiled from sight, they moulder 'neath the
 sod
In life their light and joyous footsteps trod.
Their forms may hover 'round our hearth-
 stones still,
But when Affection dies Remembrance will!

Long years ago there stood above the mill,
There, where the highway sweeps around the
 hill,

A dingy structure. Here the law's delay
In solemn majesty held sovereign sway.
Within, a rusty stove, some musty books,—
Blind guides through labyrinths of quirks and
　　crooks ! —
An oaken table, crazy, drunken chair ;
How fumes of mouldy age perfumed the air !
The floor was worn with half a century's
　　tread,
What cobwebs draped the plaster overhead !
The walls, they've known, like battlements,
　　the jars
Of shafts forensic, speeded for the stars.
The schemes confided to their dull, deaf
　　ears !
Had walls but tongues ! Would hearts not
　　quake with fears ?

The justice, crusty, formal, sage, severe,
Wore golden spectacles, had one deaf ear ;

His head was bowed beneath the books he
    knew;
The jewels of his heart he seldom shew.
The widow here and orphan found a friend:
Did not his shoulders 'neath their burdens
    bend?
See, where he walks, as silent as the trees!
Who doffs his hat to him who seldom sees?
Some say his soul's as dry as prairie dust;
Some say the toils of love he ne'er would
    trust;
And others tell about a sister's son,
With whom he's seen sometimes in sport to
    run
And frolic like a noisy, roistering boy,
Enamoured of a dog or some new toy.

Still others say there was a haughty maid
(Now 'neath the maples in the churchyard
    laid)

Who once — when suns were bright and skies
    were blue,
When cheeks were red and hearts seemed
    always true,
When youth's bright bow of promise hung
    above —
The merry-hearted student dared to love.
Betimes, on moonlit evenings, were they seen
Upon the silver river's shimmering sheen,
Or strolling o'er the mead, along the shore
Where all is solitude save ocean's roar.
'Tis said that wild caprice dispelled her vow ;
'Tis said her haughty spirit would not bow
Beneath the yoke of his imperious will.
When death the bow-string broke, he loved
    her still ;
And now that winter bows his snow-white
    head,
When darkness folds the earth in sleep, 'tis
    said,

He walks beside her grave, repentant man!
And seeks, betimes, such comfort as he can.

'Tis Autumn.　Now　the　bending,　bearded
　　grain
Is　threshed　and　winnowed,　loaded　on　the
　　wain;
By plodding oxen to the mill 'tis drawn,
And　ground　to　flour　or　changed　for　golden
　　corn.
'Tis　now　is　seen　the　full-mowed,　bursting
　　barn;
The thrifty housewife spinning stocking yarn;
Now　red-cheeked　apples　groan　beneath　the
　　press;
The flying shuttle weaves gray winter's dress.
'Tis now the rustling leaves, in eddying waves,
Seek, in sequestered nooks, inconstant graves;
'Tis now, in carols, whispering breezes sing
The harvesting of hopes, sown thick in spring;

In gathering conclave, chattering birds delight
Our friendly ears before their southern flight ;
And oft the furtive line across the sky
Bespeaks the blue-billed widgeon shooting by.

'Tis now — of fairest, loveliest scenes the
    best ! —
The husbandman, his yearly toilings blest,
Around the bending board his thanks returns
To Him who blest the crop his labor earns.
Who has not seen the farmer's happy home,
Surpassing all beneath earth's azure dome ?
His sunburnt face, his rosy, blithesome wife,
His children bubbling o'er with sparkling life ?
When darkness floats across the face of
    earth,
No anxious goblins dance around his hearth.
The sun and air their legacies bequeath,
Health's freshest garland round his brow in-
    wreathe !

Where, where, is found a scene of such delight
As greets the eye upon an autumn night,
When,— day's drear labor done, the cattle
  fed,—
Before their tired limbs retire to bed,
The father, mother, children, all enjoy
An hour of rest,— rest free from care's alloy ?
Before the blazing log the settle stands ;
The younger list to tales of fairy lands ;
The eldest boy, his mother's bright-eyed pride,
Whose prayers have sought his careless steps
  to guide
In wisdom's ways, upon a book intent,
Is wrestling with his evening's stubborn stent.
While the embers flicker and the taper burns,
The mother's frugal hand the flax-wheel turns.
Beside her Alice, grave, some garment mends,
Betimes a look of sympathy extends
To a neighbor's son, whose furtive glances
  seek

That Hope's bright blush may visit his wan
    cheek,
While with her father, round the hearth, he
    speaks
Of the harvest and the tempest's recent freaks.

The clock strikes nine, the children's hour for
    bed ;
The sire takes down the book, with reverent
    head,
From off the shelf. All work is laid aside.
He reads, in tones dispelling worldly pride,
" The Lord my Shepherd is ; with generous will
He leads through pastures green, by waters
    still ;
I walk through death's dim vale, and fear no
    harm ;
Thou art my rod, my staff, my trusting arm."
Then, kneeling all in reverent circle round
The shrine in every pious household found,

The father begs with fervent, trusting zeal
For sweet contentment, whether woe or weal,
For grace, for health, for pardon for each
    sin,
Life's choicest blessings upon all their kin.

'Tis homes like these that made our fathers
    strong,
That steeled their hearts to wrestle with the
    wrong.
When faith in God is from her banner torn,
Our land is of her giant power shorn.
'Twas faith in man that set a nation free,
The Pilgrims guided 'cross the raging sea;
In war, this shibboleth inspired the brave,
And steeled their hearts to dare a traitor's
    grave.
It made our modern Cincinnatus great;
Held fast with giant hand the helm of state;
Ay! made Columbia our patron saint,

Her glowing skies with Freedom's flag did
    paint !
When God, when Faith in Man, are spurned
    with scorn,
And sons like sons of old no longer born,
When sweet Simplicity wears mourning
    shrouds,
While arrant Wealth stalks through admiring
    crowds,
When cravens spurn the prize of high endeavor,
Then sinks our country's sun, sinks, sets, for-
    ever.

THE FOUNTAIN.

WITHIN a crowded city
  A fountain may be seen :
Three little sisters gave it,
  That fount of dancing sheer

Upon its base the legend
  Their generous impulse tells,—
How Love like sparkling nectar
  From childish heart-springs wells !

Ere morning gilds the steeples,
  Ere Commerce crowds the square,
The farmers with the bounties
  Of early June are there.

What lusty peals of laughter !
　What rustic shouts resound,
While drink their panting horses
　Or, eager, paw the ground !

When gleam the rays of noon-day,
　Here comes the lolling hound,
Here sporting with its splashes
　Are laughing children found.

Night brings the merry minstrel,
　The jolly beggar-throng,
Who all with glad hosannas
　The gift enshrine in song.

THE SOLDIER'S DREAM.

IT is the ninth of April, a grand historic day,
The day the South surrendered,— how Time
   has flown away!
The room is veiled in midnight ; no sound dis-
   turbs the air
Except the breath of anguish, the footfall of
   fond care.

The savior of his country lies face to face with
   Death,
Whose lean and icy fingers constrain his chok-
   ing breath;
A panoramic vision illumes his dreaming
   sight,
'Tis the vision of a lifetime, a life from dawn
   till night: —

A child of sunny summers, beside his mother's
    knee ;
A youth of earnest purpose his half-shut eye-
    lids see ;
A grave and silent soldier, the pride of the
    parade ;
He rides as did young Cortez 'gainst Mon-
    tezuma's blade.

He sees a sun-burnt farmer within a rural
    home,
Beside a blazing hearthstone, whose fancies
    never roam
Except where boon-companions, with pipes
    and foaming beer,
Tell tales of wild adventure, sing songs of
    hearty cheer.

But hark! the bugle calleth! Its clarions
    wake the farms,—
"Your country is in danger! To arms! My
    sons, to arms!"

The roads are black with soldiers, their bris-
    tling bayonets gleam,
A hundred thousand marching, as flows a
    mountain stream !

But now the dreamer's vision descries a bat-
    tle-field ;
He hears the cannon echo, he sees battalions
    yield ;
He sees the blue-coats rally, he sees the gray-
    coats fall,
The ghastly dead and dying, the " stars and
    bars " their pall.

Along the queen of rivers, against her trem-
    bling shore,
Volcanic flames are belching and volleying
    thunders roar !
Hot shot and shell are crashing, while lurid
    smoke and flame
Are from a fortress leaping,— a fortress known
    to fame !

Again the picture changes. The Capitol is
    seen,
Where rolls the broad Potomac through fra-
    grant evergreen ;
Not now fraternal kindness disports in festive
    garb,
But brother armed 'gainst brother spurs on his
    fiery barb.

Brigades and solid squadrons are marching
    out of camp,
He hears their stirring music, he hears their
    sturdy tramp ;
The Wilderness the arena, a nation's life the
    prize ;
Their shibboleth is, "Richmond!" Hear,
    hear, their battle cries !

For days, aye, weeks, embattled, repulsed, de-
    feated, slain,
As sands restrain old Ocean, their ranks roll
    back again,

Till rising, surging higher, with loud, resound-
    ing roar,
The foaming, bounding billows sweep o'er the
    crumbling shore.

Now he sees a planter's dwelling in Appomat-
    tox's vale ;
The earth is piled in breastworks, 'tis rent with
    iron hail.
What villages of canvas ! What hosts in blue
    and gray !
Why halt those gleaming columns? What
    means this wild dismay?

Why parley yonder chieftains, those heroes
    full a score ?
They're the victors and the vanquished. Thank
    God ! The war is o'er.
"This olive branch shall shield you. The sun
    of peace shall shine.
This flag," so says the victor, "its ægis still is
    thine."

No lion tone and bearing! No eagle's eye of
    pride!
As modest as a school-boy, the conqueror seeks
    to hide
His speechless joy of triumph by generous
    act and word.
He feeds the conquered army! The beggar
    seems the lord.

The reveille has sounded. 'Twill never sound
    again.
For days, in martial splendor, three hundred
    thousand men,
From Vicksburg and from Shiloh, Antietam
    and the Sea,
From Shenandoah's Valley, from Gettysburg's
    green lea;

Those cannoneers of ruin, that hurricane of
    horse,
With Pestilence behind them, with Famine in
    their course;

Those, those, when Pickett's cohorts were
    charging wave on wave,
That stood like granite ledges, the bravest of
    the brave,

With drums, and banners flying, with triumph
    in each eye,
In grand review are marching.   He sees them
    passing by,—
He sees, as saw Napoleon, from that triumphal
    arch,
That night in phantom phalanx, his splendid
    heroes march,—

The heroes of Marengo, the lions of the Nile,
The barefoot, Russian legions that could at
    Famine smile,
The guard that ne'er surrendered, Murat and
    Soult and Ney,
The hounds that hunted Blucher, but threw
    the world away.

How like a shield of crimson that sun of
    Austerlitz!
What ghastly, gory phantom before our hero
    flits?
Do not a nation's idols who lead her lovers
    well,
Shall they not hold her sceptre, in halls of
    purple dwell?

Have not the hoary Ages their victors loved
    to crown?
Shall not the flaming falchion still win sublime
    renown?
They echoed, we'll re-echo, the glories of the
    brave,
And all, a grateful country, bedew the soldier's
    grave.

THE GRAVE OF EMERSON.

In Sleepy Hollow, 'neath the pines
    That breathe a dirge of tender sighs,
Where Spring her first fond tendril twines,
    The seer of Concord lies.

Two forest monarchs, sentinels
    To guard his grave, disciples find;
The breath of fresh-cut immortelles
    Suggests his living mind.

Why carve that name upon a stone,
    The spot with rail or hedges bound?
The pilgrim, from earth's furthest zone,
    Will find this beacon mound!

Thou, Nature, thou wilt guard his grave,
  As thou hast yonder shrine so long;
Thy princely lovers, true and brave,
  Romance and Delphic Song.

IMMORTALITY.

PALE death steals o'er us as a spectral cloud
At eventide steals o'er Monadnock's height,
Its form enfolding in a fleecy cloud,
Its grandeur veiling from our straining sight ;
Yet sunset crowns its head.   No storms have
  bowed
Its towering majesty.   Its crown of light
Gleams now more bright that mists conceal
  from view
Its form suspended in yon veil of blue.

INGRATITUDE.

KIND Norah tried, the summer long,
  Tried in her kind, delightful way,
To make love's tendrils grow more strong
  Around two sweethearts, gone astray.

Did she not list to each complaint?
  Did she not soothe Inconstance' woe?
Alas! as waning love grew faint,
  What thanks had she? — "Why did you so?"

IMPECUNIAS.

How poverty will dwarf the mind,
  Dry up the well-springs of the heart!
It makes the noblest seem unkind,
  And act the cynic's part.

The rose that grows beneath the shade,
  Without the sun, the breezes' breath,
How soon, alas, its glories fade!
  It lives a life-in-death.

The lion, chain him in a cage,
  When he would roam as free as air,
Does he not gnaw his heart with rage,
  Sigh for his forest lair?

ALICE.

SHALL I ever dare to tell you
  With what trembling steps I went,
On that summer eve to see you,
  On my anxious errand bent?

How I conned my message over,
  As a school-boy does a sum,
That no words should seem a rover,
  Nor like timid rabbits run?

With what throbbing heart I waited,
  Ere I dared my favor ask,
Till the stammering words, belated,
  Seemed an awkward rustic's task?

Never shall I dare — no, never —
　　Tell how sweet those moments seemed,
Tell how loath I was to sever
　　Joys for which I long had dreamed.

When Sleep kissed your downy pillow,
　　Shall I ever dare disclose
That I waited 'neath your window
　　Till the laughing moon arose,—

Rose and saw me 'neath your casement,
　　Watching your pale taper's ray,
Glorying in my self-abasement,
　　Wishing the swift stars would stay?

Restless, heartsick, now I'm tossing,
　　Tossing on my bed to-night,
Hopes and fears together crossing
　　O'er my half-awakened sight !

Fearing lest your kind refusal
  Meant for me a mild rebuke,
Hoping on a reperusal
  Your blind meaning I mistook.

April suns and April showers
  Shade the lowland, crown the hill,
Cloud and lighten lovers' hours,
  Always do, and always will.

WASHINGTON'S BIRTHDAY.

BELLS are ringing,
Children singing,
To commemorate one man's name!
Cannon resounding,
Echoes rebounding,
To perpetuate Washington's fame!

Freedom obtained,
A republic gained,
A cynosure set to the world;
Virtue triumphant,
Courage exultant,
A national banner unfurled!

A VALENTINE.

How the frown that my hasty word brought
   Like a spectre has haunted the night!
When again you, my love, I have caught,
   From my arms you shall never take flight!

Did not clouds often darken the sun,
   Should we not e'en of Nature's face tire?
Did not discords with harmonies run,
   Should we still love the strains of the lyre?

When we parted last night in a pet,
   At the words I so carelessly spoke,
I ne'er thought I should pine with regret;
   But I now from my trance have awoke.

And before the whole world is awake,
  While the birds their sweet orisons sing,
A true love-knot of roses I'll take,
  And into your lattice I'll fling.

Should they chance on your couch to alight,
  May they twine round your golden-fleck'd
      hair ;
May they catch your awakening sight,
  If your dreams do not say they are there.

OPHELIA'S LOVE.

MAD for love of thee,
The chords of life distraught!
The string that held the bow
Has snapped!   'Twas drawn too taut!
  My mind, a raging sea
  Of fierce delirium,
  Sings in wild despair
  Its own sad requiem!

A MADRIGAL.

'Tis rapture after pain
Your too proud heart to gain;
To fold you in my arms,
To revel in your charms,
And know your love is true.
Your melting eyes of blue
Look fondly into mine,
Intoxicate like wine!

The love-light in your face,
Your long-withheld embrace,
This first, soft, lingering kiss,
Oh! sweetest of all bliss!
The promise of your heart
Till Eternity us part,
Make days hereafter seem
One everlasting dream!

EMERSON.

PROSE poet of the adventurous mind and heart,
Brave guide through paths of dim philosophy,
Stern moralist! Thou from the Church didst
    part,
When creeds had died of pious atrophy.
Thou, Druid-like, took Nature for thy chart,
Interpreting her dark poligraphy ;
Believing Christ's dear Testament was meant
To be a solace, not a discontent.

TO ANNIE.

You ask me why your swain has fled?
  Why eyes that glow with rapture
  No bright reflection capture,
Only a "look like burnished lead"?

The bird that loves the mountain air,
  That soars on Freedom's pinions,
  Disdains pale Fashion's minions,
Aye, takes his flight to escape her snare.

DIANA.

QUEEN of the games! Fair mistress of the
    bow!
Sovereign of all who wield the sportsman's
    dart!
Before thy feet thy worshipper would throw
A laurel plucked pursuing your dear art.

He owes to thee the skill that nerves his arm,
    The bounding stride that covers leagues
        with ease,
Sweet health, surpassing e'en the Houri's
      charm :
    Here, here, fair queen, behold him on his
        knees!
With pious gratitude, he kisses e'en your robe,
More proud, more rich, perhaps, than if he
    owned the globe.

THE DELIGHTS OF LABOR.

WERE Truth a wild gazelle
Bounding o'er hill and dell,
Could I ensnare, the springe I'd tear,
Aye, once again embrace
The pleasure of the chase.

'Tis hope inspires our toil !
Hope gilds drear labor's moil !
What tears of blight, like dews of night,
Despairing eyelids shed,
When Elysian dreams have fled !

A RETROSPECT.

I.

FAIR Hudson ! on thy palisades there stood,
  One glorious autumn morn, a youth and
    maid,
Who scanned, with pensive eye, thy silent flood.
  They seemed the wood-nymphs of your ever-
    glade :
His sun-burnt face bespoke an Indian brave,
  Who had left his bark upon your tangled
    bank ;
Her eyes reflected your bright, azure wave ;
  Her blooming cheeks told tales of sires
    who drank
The nectar Norman nobles sipped from rock-
    cleft wells ;
Of knightly chivalry her stately carriage tells.

II.

As there they stood, a boat swung round the
  cliff,
  And bowed its gleaming prow towards the
    shore ;
The tide ran strong, deep-laden was the skiff,
  The boatman toiled and tugged with lusty
    oar.
Now scarce she moves! Ah, now some
    Triton's hand
  Drags back, along the shore, her leaden
    keel !
But see ! whose form is that upon the strand ?
  Whose voice ?   His wife's !   His sinews
    now are steel !
When this these gazers saw, Love lighted tell-
    tale eyes,
And here and thus each won a life-long prize.

LOVE'S SACRIFICE.

TRUE Love and Friendship met one morn,
  When both were blithe and cares were few,
When Pleasure filled Youth's golden horn,
  And Nature wore her loveliest hue.

How gayly, swiftly sped the day!
  What elfin sports! What shouts of glee!
They chased the sportive sunshine's ray,
  Played hide-and-seek round rock and tree.

But when, from dusky pinions, Night
  The chilling dews of darkness showered,
Then Friendship slept, poor thoughtless wight!
  While Love his bed with violets flowered.

A LAMENT.

HE has laid his burden down! At last he
    sleeps!
  Those weary days, those wasting nights, are
    o'er;
The Nation bows its stricken head, and weeps!
  Could nature, feeble nature, suffer more?

Around his grave shall mourning thousands
    stand,
  As long as men love faith and manly worth;
His name a household word throughout a
    land
  That honors high endeavor more than birth.

'Tis Learning mourns a lover, who ne'er knew
  A holier fount than her Pierian spring;

'Tis Charity that mourns a suitor true,
  Who brought the gifts that faith in man
    could bring.

Yes, Statesmanship stands here, with head
      bowed down,
  And Friendship with Religion, hand in hand ;
And Eloquence has brought her laurel crown ;
  While lowly, sun-burnt toilers of the land,

A weeping concourse, 'round his bier proclaim,
  " A noble life excels a diadem " ;
E'en sceptred princes join the wide acclaim,
  And swell the chorus of his requiem !

His brilliant life repeats the sounding story,
  The legend told of Fame's enchanted halls :
There is no royal road that leads to glory,
  By birthright no one scales her sapphire
    walls.

The Chian minstrel and the Thracian slave
  Parnassus' splendid heights and groves sur-
      vey ;
Aye, hand in hand, with stately Cæsar, wave
  Immortal garlands, tread its golden way !

The mother mourns. But, oh ! the faithful wife !
  She loved the school-boy with his ruddy
      face;
She held the lamp that lighted manhood's
      strife ;
  Care's wrinkled forehead smoothed with
      tender grace.

How oft the fruit is blasted by the frost !
  She nurses now, alone, her bitter grief,
Recalls the sleepless nights this bauble cost,
  With sad remembrance for her sole relief.

As rainbows fade, so fades a splendid name !
  Since God pronounced the primal curse of
      toil,

Though Wisdom points the hand of scorn at
    Fame,
Philosophers still burn their blood for oil,

Poets still haunt the shores of Fancy's realm,
    For fame the sculptor begs one hour of life,
The patriot holds, through blinding blasts, the
    helm,
    The soldier fights where fiercest swells the
    strife.

But what the seer, prophetic, oft has told
    This lonely widow's heart now knows is
    true ;
These thundering words have down the ages
    rolled,—
    " Shadows we are, and shadows we pursue."

PRIDE.

HAVE you ever seen the tulip
　　Hold aloft his haughty head,
Gorgeous, grand, imperial tulip,
　　Rising from his emerald bed?

When the breezes chase each other,
　　Bend the daisies, pansies, down,
Bend to earth in filial worship,
　　Does the tulip bow his crown?

Flower of pride!　Gay flower of passion!
　　Emblem of monarchal will!
Born to shine where courtly fashion
　　Reigns in splendid households still.

ALFREDA.

THE churchyard is spectral and dreary,
  The village enshrouded in sleep ;
There kneels, where a mother lies buried,
  A maiden, who came here to weep.

" Forgive my entreaty, dear mother !
  Forgive me, as I do, our shame !
But hear my poor heart throb in anguish,
  And tell me my own father's name ! "

The greensward returns her no answer :
  The body has mouldered to dust ;
But the spirit, on airy wings wafted,
  Has flown to the realms of the just.

BEATRICE.

PROUD and imperious, passionless and chaste ;
Red lips, like ruddy coral, without taste.

FOR A LADY'S ALBUM.

THE hand that framed the Universe,
That reared Green-Mountain's storm-clad
    dome,
Has fashioned, too, these hills and dells
For Pleasure's sylvan home.

Let not, I pray, the hand of Time
Erase, as Stillness smooths the sea,
The happy, peaceful, sunset-hours
In Eden spent with thee !

MOUNT DESERT, August, 1883.

TIME CANNOT DISENCHANT.

You never said you loved me, but you were so
    very kind ;
Your eyes so full of feeling, and reflecting
    your bright mind.

My aspirations pleased you, my faintest wish
    was thine,
We were so sympathetic that your every wish
    was mine.

Your blush was so responsive, if I praised
    your brilliant beauty ;
Our hearts seemed so enchanted, there was
    nothing seemed a duty.

Were not our days like Eden, when we wan-
dered by the brooks ?
Our days sped by so swiftly, there was never
need of books.

Were not the nights Elysian, when we wan-
dered by the sea,
The faithful stars above us as we murmured
poetry?

Were eyelids ever drowsy, with your face beside my heart?
As speeds a weaver's shuttle, so came the day
to part !

Ah ! yes, the summer ended ! We both returned to town,—
You to your far-off city, and I to my books
bound down !

But whene'er I went to see you, in your charm-
ing poet-home,
Was not your mother gracious, that she left us
all alone?

But distance stood between us! Yes, old
Time held up his hands!
Base Mammon shook his gray locks. All, all,
restrained the bands!

How slowly dragged the winter! Now, June
brings back the day
When weary, dreary toilers from dun cities
flee away,

To find surcease from labor, let fond Fancy
roam awhile,
As sea-gulls do at sunset round the cliffs of
Desert Isle.

Fair isle! Thy coves and grottoes, thy shores,
    hereafter seem,
As Sestos to Leander, a foretaste of love's
    dream.

POOR TABBY.

"HAVE you, sir, seen poor Tabby?"
  This morning asked a child,
This bitter morning, early,
  In earnest accents wild.

"The ground is hard and frozen,
  'Tis blanketed with snow!
My Tabby was so feeble
  Her feet could hardly go!

"Last night my cruel brother,
  Last night, unknown to me,
He says he brought and left her
  Beside this lonely tree.

" Will Tabby not be hungry ?
  Poor thing ! Will she not die,
With none but heartless Winter
  To hear her homeless cry ? "

The sobbing words she murmured
  My pity scarce believed ;
And yet, 'tis true, her brother
  Her pet's sad death conceived.

THE GOLDEN DAY.

ONE day among these changing years
  Glows with a golden light,
Amidst the smiles, the frequent tears,
  The sunshine and the night.

It was in April.   'Twas the spring
  Of life and hope and love ;
And she who taught these lips to sing,
  Who taught these feet to rove,

Through Concord meadows roamed with me,
  That Mecca of the mind,
Where first our banner of the free
  Was given to the wind.

Our step was frolicsome and light
    As thoughtless lambs at play :
We romped and laughed from morn till night,—
    O happy, happy day !

We strolled along the flowering lea,
    And picked the violet ;
We strayed by Walden's placid sea,
    With gems of emerald set.

We floated down the silver stream,
    Toward the silver sea :
How gorgeous was that youthful dream !
    What buoyant health and glee !

We trod the famous battle-field
    Where fought the minute-men,
Where farmers learned the sword to wield,
    And died to live again.

Did not our bosoms swell with pride?
  Did not we bless the dead,
And wish we, too, like them, had died
  Upon a martyr's bed?

We saw where weird Romance had dwelt,
  We kissed the very earth
Where Transcendentalism felt
  The travail of its birth.

Our thoughts were filled with fairy dreams
  Of love and fond renown : —
What's this before our eyesight gleams?
  Is this a laurel crown?

'Twas here I wove of violets
  A garland for my love :
Far richer, far, than coronets,
  It lives in courts above.

'Twas here I kissed her ruddy lips
　The first fond kiss of love.
The bee that June's first honey sips
　Has not such treasure-trove.

'Twas here I told her of my love,
　With fervent, faltering tongue ;
Our vows are registered above ;
　The breeze her answer sung.

Below the stream of Life there flows
　Another stream, called Death :
The first with buds of fragrance blows ;
　The last, a barren heath.

She scarcely lived our honeymoon,
　But 'twas such ecstasy !
Before her clock of life struck noon,
　'Twas all a memory.

I stand within the porch of death,
Her sainted form appears,
But vanishes, like spirit-breath,
In bitter, blinding tears.

A THRENODY.

(Written on revisiting the deserted home of George
William Phillips, at Saugus.)

How often have I reverently trod
This sea-girt intervale and velvet sod,—
As level as fair Cana's threshing floor!
Oft seen the cattle browsing round the door,
Sweet children sporting on the emerald lawn,
Oft heard the songsters heralding the dawn,
The babbling brook along the flowery mead,
The zephyrs bowing down the stately reed!
How proud was I to grasp his cordial hand,—
Warm with the noblest blood in all the land!
To list, beside his hospitable fire,
To words as sweet as ever minstrel's lyre!

When last I stood beside yon wicket gate,
I came to mourn the cruel shaft of fate.
The brother,* — he who held a realm in awe
With thunders fulminating Sinai's law;
Who led, from Egypt, Afric's dusky slave;
Who stood triumphant o'er Secession's grave,
While gathering lowly myriads round his knee
To teach, for love, the Vedas of the free;—
He met me there, his heart dissolved in tears;
Bereft of one who, throughout threescore years,
Had stayed his hands, as Aaron did of old
The hands that guided Israel's wandering fold.

Now stalks the stranger o'er these lonely fields,
Whose soil its incense with reluctance yields;
Irreverent urchins sport beneath the shade
Where schemes to break a people's chains were
    laid;
Grim Sacrilege sits, raven-like, on high,
And from yon gable mocks the passer-by;

    * Wendell Phillips.

While Desecration tears this altar down
Which Freedom's lovers honored with a crown.

O Time, what changes have thy fingers
    wrought!
What ruin thou, along thy track, hast brought!
Thy vandal hand has laid Palmyra low,
Has made the furze o'er Carthagena grow,
Yes, razed the Imperial City's mammoth
    walls!
Before thy sledge the Coliseum falls,
Alhambra's stately turrets kiss the sod,
Gray Pisa's tower trembles at thy nod,
Great Necker's Palace crumbles into dust,
Proud Cheops wastes with thy corroding rust;
While stern Niagara's awful, thundering roar
Shakes Earth's foundation, gnaws its crum-
    bling shore!
Old states and empires fade, like mist, away,
The firmament acknowledges thy sway.

When Change has wrought its wasting impress
    here,
Is it strange that man survives his short-lived
    year?
How sad, when Death's relentless hand we feel,
The blow is struck no necromance can heal,
The world moves on, nor mourns our hapless
    lot!
How soon, alas, our faces are forgot!

ALCÆUS AND SAPHIA.

ALCÆUS loved a fickle maid
  With all the fervor of his heart :
He thought that she his love repaid,
  He thought they ne'er should part.

But Saphia fair was like the dove
  That loves with other doves to toy,
Too young to know the worth of love,
  Her heart was shy and coy.

Alcæus could not brook the smiles
  His sweetheart showered on other swains ;
His jealous eye rebelled ere whiles,
  Rebelled against his pains.

When Saphia saw the silent grief
   Her coquetries, so thoughtless, caused,
She fain would fly to his relief ;
   In her caprice she paused,

And tried by every grace she knew,
   By kindnesses he loved the most,
To hold the heart her beauty drew ; —
   She only held its ghost !

The bird, once flown, may not return ;
   The swain, once gone, may stay away ;
The maid from this who cannot learn
   May learn some other day.

AT ANCHOR.

OUR shallop now sleeps in the bay!
 The gale that has furrowed the waves,
That has deluged the deck with their spray,
 Has returned to its home in the caves.

Far richer than rubies the rest
 That follows a boisterous day,
When we know we have struggled our best,
 And the clouds of despair roll away!

TO A LADY UPON HER BIRTHDAY.

" 'TIS true that I am growing old,
　　That silver threads entwine my hair,
That Father Time — his heart is cold ! —
　　Must set his stamp on young and fair ;
That Grace, my child, is woman grown,
Now takes the place was once my own.

" Ah ! yes, 'tis true !　To-day I add
　　Another to the many years
That have been happy, have been sad,
　　Whose page is wet with bitter tears
For others' woes besides my own :
But a merry face I have always shown ! "

These whispered words I seemed to hear
  The South-wind sigh, as once I went
Along a crowded city's pier.
  What answer, think you, back I sent?
"How few, how few, till strength is spent,
Know what that mother's murmur meant!"

A TALK WITH A TOAD.

WHILE raking down the garden lawn,
   I spied a little toad :
She sat beneath a bush forlorn,
   Beside the gravelled road.

I said, "What makes your face so sad,
   This bright, sweet summer day,
When heart of man and beast is glad,
   This morn, a-making hay?"

"We toads," said she, "have sorrows, too,
   As great as we can bear :
As large for us as yours for you
   Is our great load of care.

"We live in pairs, the same as you ;
  We love each other, too :
Just now, some great, big, ugly shoe
  Has crushed ' Smug's ' toe in two.

" What, what to do, where, where to go,
  I cannot, cannot think :
Sir, what will cure my sweetheart's toe ?
  What can, what can he drink ?

" There's rosemary, one nurse prescribes ;
  There's wormwood, says another;
A third, Miss Wiseacre, decides
  That plantain cured her brother.

" My little mate sits, crazed with pain,
  Beneath yon willow tree :
What herb, sir, shall a toad obtain,
  When doctors disagree ? "

MOUNT DESERT.

YE castled crags along the coast of Maine!
Ye giant cliffs, whose feet the billows lave,
Whose wind-swept currents sing the sea's re-
   frain!
The eagle's eyrie and the smuggler's cave
Are all the homes thy fastnesses allow!

Thy domes and pinnacles gleam like some
   gem
Upon the swelling bosom of the sea;
Thy forehead wears a glittering diadem,
Our eyes afar some new Atlantis see,
Some new Gibraltar greet gray Neptune's bow.

Here sits the Avalanche! Here foaming
    brooks
Leap dazzling cliffs or dance along the
    dell!
Here shadows haunt still lakes and sylvan
    nooks!
Here Fancy's fauns and sportive wood-nymphs
    dwell,
All Nature wears the livery of Eden!

Ye mountains bold, who rear your cloud-girt
    heads,
Serene, sublime, from out a boundless sea;
Whose seamed, embattled sides are water-
    sheds,
Down which the torrent bounds, unbridled,
    free,
Through wild ravines, to yon cliff-crested
    haven!

When in your presence how the soul expands,
In adoration of the Almighty Cause!
Thought soars, on airy wings, to distant lands;
Its pinions sweep the stars! They note the
     laws
That hold in subtile chains yon circling
     spheres!

From your bald peaks the village can be seen,
Half hid 'neath golden vapors of the morn;
The drowsy cottage, peering through the green,
Within whose shadows Happiness was born,
Whose peaceful groves Remembrance so en-
     dears.

MARGUERITE.

You ask me why I lead this life,
So wild, so full of bitter strife?
Why I am not a happy wife?
    You wish to know my story?

You think that beauty such as mine
Should not be spoilt by men and wine,
But round some cottage door should twine,
    Like some sweet morning-glory?

You wonder why I never try
To save the lustre of mine eye?
You wonder why I long to die,
    To end this long carousal?

Why all this glitter has no charm,
My hectic flush gives no alarm,
What earlier sin occurred to harm
  A holier espousal?

It might have been !— except for one
Whose smile was like the morning sun,
Towards which the climbing woodbines run
  To blossom in his favor.

A twelve-month since my mother died :
'Twas he who kissed my tears aside,
'Twas he with sweet caresses tried
  To lighten sorrow's labor.

He seemed, aye, felt, as sad as I :
How oft a tear bedimmed his eye !
How oft, how patiently, he'd try
  Grief's gloomy gnomes to frighten !

He carried flowers to her grave :
How tender was he ! oh, how brave !
When Anguish whelmed me like a wave,
  His smiles my load would lighten !

Ah, blame me, sir, if now you can :
His kindness every wish outran,
He made each dreary day a span,—
  Those days that last forever !

AFTER THE STORM.

Our shallop glides over the seas,
  Glides straight in the eye of the sun ;
When blown by the whispering breeze,
  How faintly her ripples run !

The Monarch of Day sinks down,
  To sleep by his consort, the Sea ;
No clouds ! No wrinkles ! No frown !
  Their breasts from anxiety free !

The winds and the storms of the day,
  That have crested old Ocean with waves,
That have christened our top-mast with spray,
  Are asleep in their desolate caves.

How sweet, how grateful, is rest,
  When Night draws the curtain of Day,
When we know we have toiled at our best,
  And wait for fond Victory's ray!

JEZEBEL.

How every honest woman's thought
Condemns the painted Jezebel,—
Condemns because her smiles are bought!
Can all her stately airs excel
The faintest blush of modest grace —
So timorous, so delicate —
That steals across a maiden's face,
That almost seems to supplicate
No eye should steal a glance of thought
Or admiration, all unsought?

Can all the treasury of wealth
That Crœsus had, that Midas sought,
Prometheus stole from heaven by stealth,—
Can all their pelf, their lucre, buy

The smile that lighted Heloïse?
The ray that shone in Clytie's eye?
The song that made the listening trees
With all their myriad leaves applaud,
When Sappho sighed across the lyre?
Why is it, when the wide world knows
The priceless worth of woman's love,
What happiness true love bestows,
Whene'er the bans are blest above,
So many wives their lives have sold,
So many maids are bought with gold?

A DREAM OF LIFE.

WHILE lying half-awake, one summer night,
My chamber scarcely lit with Cynthia's light;
While Silence floats along the breathless air,
No sound, except the clock behind the stair
That ticks the tardy time with tiring din;
While airy night-thoughts fairy fancies spin,—
I see two lovers on a silvery eve
The doorway of an ivied cottage leave.
They wend their slow and pensive way
Along a wooded road.   What bird-like lay
Is this that floats upon the fluttering breeze?
'Tis soft as evening's zephyr 'mong the trees!
'Tis like the whisper of Æolia's lyre!
Or like the vespers of some convent choir,

When cloisters listen to the curfew's sound,
As Darkness creeps along the dew-sprent
    ground !

What youthful grace ! what firm, elastic tread !
An athlete's figure, and a princely head !
His eye, his mien, his manly carriage, say,—
"I know no thoughts that fear the light of
    day.
Hope is my star ! She guides the eagle's
    flight ;
She guides the chamois up the Alpine height !"

The maid is lithe and graceful as a swan.
Why seems her step so languid, face so
    wan ?
Ah ! 'tis long vigils by her mother's side,
These duties, Frailty never should have tried !
To leave the suffering bedside for a while,
To walk beside her lover, watch his smile,

To hear the rippling music of his voice ;
To know that she is jewel of his choice,
Queen of his thoughts by day and dreams by
      night,—
'Tis such a boon, so sweet, such fond delight,
Her wistful thoughts forget the pallid shade
And wasting form upon the pallet laid.

The panorama changes.   Moving on,
It now discovers true love's wooing won.
Behold! the lights are gleaming in the church,
The guests assembled!   In their choir-perch,
The village belles, enrobed in downy white
And dove-like modesty,— entrancing sight ! —
Chorus the legend of the love-lorn knight
Who, in the tourney, won his long-loved wight.
The wedding march the fluted organ speeds,
While Cupid to the altar Psyche leads.
On wings unseen, 'midst soft, admiring eyes,
I hear their vows borne upward to the skies,—

Those spirit-bonds that bind a man and wife
Till death shall cut the silken cord of life !

The ghostly phantoms change again.   In
    dream,
The glories of a rustic mansion gleam.
There sits a stately matron in the door :
'Tis she, in youthful bloom, I saw of yore !
Around her knees, fair children are at play,
Their ringlets golden in the sunset's ray,
Their eyes aglow with deep poetic fire,—
Can sport, can frolic, e'er such sinews tire ?

Who's this I see beneath the lengthening
    shade ? —
Night's dusky fingers on the landscape laid ?
Who sits beside yon sparkling, babbling brook,
On which his thoughts are fixed as 'twere a
    book ?

A pensive, gray-haired man : he writes in song
Its murmuring music as it sings along.
Ah ! yes, 'tis he !   Pale Thought has drawn the
     lines
That mark the toiler in her mystic mines;
Has bowed the form that once was so erect,
But stamped him with the seal of her elect.
Yes : boyhood's dream of fancy is fulfilled,
He has won the glittering prize Ambition
     willed.
But ask if what is gained is worth the cost,
Is worth the servitude, the pleasure lost?
If, now the cup is drained, the wine, the lees,
If on the bottom still a pearl he sees?
If, like mirage across the desert seen,
Youth's day-dream, now, is not delusive sheen?

Another picture steals across the sight,
Portrays the drama's ending, — Death and
     Night.

The gathering darkness shades a grassy mound
Within a surging city's burial-ground,
Where bustling thousands pass, with scarce a
    thought
How little all their feverish toil has brought.
I see upon a mouldering slab a name
The country once has garlanded with fame,
His presence hailed with rapt, admiring eye ;
A generation bowed as he passed by.
But now yon curious traveller stands alone,
And reads with careless eye the crumbling
    stone,
With naught but mild surprise upon his face
That so much grandeur fills this narrow space.

Ye gorgeous sepulchres, how frail ye seem !
Is not the pageantry of Babylon a dream ?
Have not Athena's glories taken flight ?
Yes !   Lonely Cheops watches out Time's
    night !

Fame's temple now my fading dream displays :
I see the names, in clear, undying rays,
Emblazoned round its walls, across its vault,—
The names of heroes, martyrs free from fault,
Of patriots, warriors, poets, sages, men
Whose genius swayed their age with tongue
    or pen.
By night obscured, by time's corrosive rust,
In cobwebbed solitude, 'midst yellow dust,
I see in fading characters the name
Of him whose dream had promised lasting fame.
Youth, wealth, child, wife, love, life, a sacrifice
To fame, that fades as rainbows from the
    skies !
Could men but know how soon the tear is dry,
How few are shed, how quick their memories
    die,
Would gilded palaces, would empty praise,
Be sought, be toiled for, weary, life-long days ?